**The GET WOKE Workbook:
Unlocking the Power in You**

©2020 by I Am A Vessel Youth Movement

Printed in the United States of America

ISBN: 978-1-7359105-2-9

Published by I Am A Vessel®
P.O. Box 693
19012 Cheltenham, Pennsylvania
www.iamavessel.com

All rights reserved. This book and the information written is a compilation of material in connection with other copyrights and trademarks belonging to I Am A Vessel. The printing and publication of this text, or any part thereof, may not be reproduced in any manner whatsoever without permission from the publisher.

Get Woke is a mandate for youth culture of today. A mandate challenging youth and young adults to open their minds and eyes to everything happening around and on the inside of themselves. I Am A Vessel would like to thank you for taking this journey towards your self discovery. We believe that from the foundations of the earth God created you for such a time. It is a time to be great, fulfilled and intentional about discovering the power that lies within you. Learn more about I Am A Vessel , self-cultivation, and our Creative pathway for life. Join the I Am A Vessel Youth Movement via our website www.iamavessel.org.

Follow us @i_am_avessel
contact us: youthmove@iamavessel.org

THIS WORKBOOK BELONGS TO:

Name: _____

Section: _____

Date: _____

Score: _____

What does Get Woke mean to you and young culture?

SUSTAINING... #GET WOKE

Get Woke: Unlocking The Power Within You.

GET WOKE
WORKBOOK

INTRODUCTION
Get woke is a tool awakening youth and provides them with a tool for life.

FOUNDATION
Foundations are the underlying principles. It is the strength and substance of something.

EXPLORATION
The prerequisite for youth to Get Woke is a journey through the unfolding of how they think.

WORTH
The productivity of youth is connected to what they value.

DIG DEEP
Digging deep is going beyond the surface to gain understanding.

EYE SURGERY
How you see goes beyond your eyesight. Therefore you must examine, protect and develop a strong vision for your future.

LEVEL UP
Leveling up is stepping up to the plate and removing all doubt and fear and become great.

NO LIMITS
Having no limits is a state of mind.

Have faith.
Find revelation.
Use strategy.
Speak Power.
Think great

LET THERE BE LIGHT

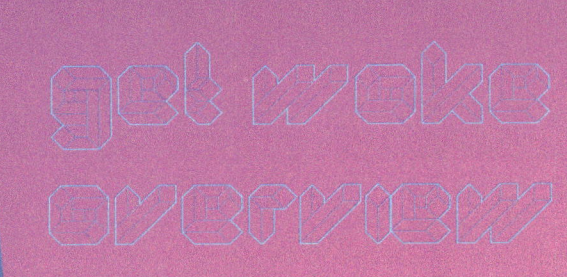

get woke overview

In your own words summarize each chapter of Get Woke.

- [ ] **INTRODUCTION**

- [ ] **FOUNDATION**

- [ ] **EXPLORATION**

- [ ] **WORTH**

GET WOKE: UNLOCKING THE POWER WITHIN YOU
#GETWOKE

☐ **DIG DEEP**

☐ **EYE SURGERY**

☐ **LEVEL UP**

☐ **NO LIMITS**

☐ **LET THERE BE LIGHT**

#GETWOKE

The parts of the book that...
WOKE ME UP!

GET WOKE REVIEW

Knowledge is Power so let's see how much you've aquired while reading Get Woke.

From the Inroduction

1) What does it mean to get woke?

2) What role does it play in sustainability of youth?

3) What are some of the crucial societal changes youth are being developed in?

4) From your perspective, how has these changes affected youth of today

5) How do you "Build Yourself?"

6) What are some materials you need to design and build your life?

7) What are the two part of who you are and why is it imperative for you to acknowledge?

8) What does your spiritual self represent?

FOUNDATION

9) What crisis happened in 2008 and how did some recover from losing everything?

10) How can that be applied to the current world circumstances of today?

11) Our foundation is super important. Why?

12) What is self-cultivation and why is it key to "Getting Woke?"

13) What is a vessel and where does the term derive from?

14) What defines who you are and why is it important to intentionally define yourself?

THIS ONE THING I CAN BE SURE OF:

> I AM A VESSEL. I HAVE A PURPOSE AND A DESTINY... THEREFORE I HAVE BEEN BLESSED WITH A PATH. ALL I NEED TO DO IS EXPLORE FROM THE INSIDE OUT.

GET WOKE: UNLOCKING THE POWER WITHIN YOU

EXPLORATION

15) Why is it imperative for youth to explore?

16) What is the purpose of expanding your mind?

17) What is culture and what role does it play in the lives of youth today?

18) What is self-cultivation and why is it key to "Getting Woke?"

19) What is the current cultural identity that youth operate in or has adopted?

20) What are the senses and how valuable are they?

21) What do the senses influence and how can they be protected?

WORTH

22) What characteristics is worth for things based on?

23) How valuable is your time and how well do you utilize it? What needs to change?

24) How should we determine our worth?

25) What are some clues about time can we find within all of God's Creation?

26) How do these elements pertain to your everyday life?

DIG DEEP

27) What does it mean to dig deep?

28) What does digging deep require and why is moving beyond the surface important?

29) What is the process for youth to dig deep and why?

30) Why is stimulation a topic for youth to consider?

31) What is the effects of overstimulation and how can youth protect themselves?

32) What are D-Perspectives and how can you put them to practice?

EYE SURGERY

33) What does the chapter "Eye Surgery" imply about youth culture?

34) How important is vision and why?

35) What is a spiritual lens and why is it necessary?

36) What is the "Power of the Lenses?"

37) What is required for youth to do in order to mature?

38) What are the 5 Vessel Lenses?

39) What power do they each hold?

40) Why are Cultural Lens different from others?

41) Name and describe the security channels.

LEVEL UP

42) What power do words and thoughts have in one's life?

43) What did the experiment by Dr. Emote conclude?

44) Define self-unity. (TM)

I got WOKE and so did my *dreams*

I Am A Vessel

45) What is the method you learned to control your emotions?

NO LIMIT

46) Who is Master P?

47) How did he create history?

48) What did he mean by "I'm a no limit soldier"?

49) What standard did he set for himself that established his wealth?

50) What is a covenant?

51) What are some covenants teens may make unknowingly?

52) What is spiritual excellence?

53) What have you learned about the human mind and spirit?

54) What have you learned about the importance of knowing who you are?

55) What ill behaviors or habits could you eliminate to elevate yourself?

56) What is faith?

57) What are the benefits of self-awareness and self-acceptance?

58) What is youth dominion?

59) What needs to be activated for youth to move past thier limits and why?

60) What needs to be activated for youth to truly move beyond thier limits and why?

61) What is revelation?

BONUS QUESTIONS

62) What is the context of Youth Intelligence in regards to "Get Woke?"

63) What do youth need to anchor themselves?

64) What are you demonstrating by saying the I Am the Vessel decree?

65) What does the I Am a Vessel pyramid represent?

66) What is the current mandate on youth culture?

KEEP GOING!

I'VE BEEN THINKING...

Free space to write, draw, and let out your thoughts.

I'VE BEEN THINKING...

I'VE BEEN THINKING...

I'VE BEEN THINKING...

I'VE BEEN THINKING...

I'VE BEEN THINKING...

I'VE BEEN THINKING...

I'VE BEEN THINKING...

I'VE BEEN THINKING...

I'VE BEEN THINKING...

I'VE BEEN THINKING...

I'VE BEEN THINKING...

I'VE BEEN THINKING...

www.ingramcontent.com/pod-product-compliance
Lightning Source LLC
Chambersburg PA
CBHW040108120526
44589CB00039B/2797